UNSEEN HAND OF GOD

UNSEEN HAND OF GOD

Lona Richard

Dedication

I dedicate this book to the Holy Spirit who inspired the cover story, giving me the revelations concerning the contents of this book.

Introduction

Thank you for picking up this book. I am writing this just for you! I may never meet you face-to-face, but God put you on my heart. I asked Him what I should tell you. He said to tell you that He is doing for you what He did for Moses: guiding, navigating, nudging, propelling, providing, protecting (throughout your life's journey).

> ***Joshua 3:7*** *And the Lord said to Joshua, "This day I will begin to exalt you in the sight of all Israel, that they may know that, as I was with Moses, so I will be with you."*

The principles in this book will apply to ANY decision, challenge, or STORM (man-made, man-induced, or nature-made) you may face in your lifetime. God wants you to know that He is guiding you through this journey. The Journey of Your Life! God is positioning and repositioning (redirecting) you every step along the way. He has ALL the answers.

> ***Psalms 121:1-2*** *I will lift up mine eyes unto the hills, from whence cometh my help. ² My help cometh from the Lord, which made heaven and earth.*

Look Up to Him from whence Your Help Cometh. He is making sure your momentum is right and orchestrating things and people all along the journey to help you and be there for you!

So why do I write this book?

We all need to be enlightened (shown) and reminded, that regardless of what we face (decisions, challenges we encounter and must overcome, or crises), that <u>God is directing us and is always sovereign in our lives.</u> He equipped us before we entered this world. We must re-evaluate our priorities. My prayer for you is that you recognize and realize everything God is telling you through the pages that follow. I look forward to meeting you someday soon. I am praying for you, even though I haven't met you yet! If you are reading this book, I am certain God is guiding you. I am cheering you on and look forward to seeing you in Heaven!

Table of Contents

Chapter One

Unseen Hand of God

In the quiet coolness of the pre-dawn morning hours, in the small village of Goshen, a woman named Jochebed is dealing with an impending brutal decision she must make. It will require her to trust God at a deeper level than ever before. That she must "let go and let God". Never in her wildest dreams had she imagined she would have to hide her newborn baby boy just to keep him alive. She never dreamed or imagined she would be required to let go of her precious baby boy so soon after his birth. His very life was dependent on the water tightness of the reed basket vessel crafted and sealed by her own hands. What a grave responsibility!

For weeks now, she has been busy until the late night hours, carefully and tightly weaving and tarring (sealing) the reed basket that will soon carry her newborn baby boy, Moses, to an unknown destination. To Safety. To the next chapter and step in his life. [1]She has chosen bulrush reeds which specifically give off an offensive odor to known predators of the Nile river (such as crocodiles and snakes). Bulrush reeds are also known for their durability (capability of withstanding both hard and soft objects). The tar she is using is pitch, a watertight sealant as coating to ensure the reed basket does not leak or sink. The inside of the reed basket is lined with bitumen which is soft, but also serves to shield the infant from the strong, offensive odor of the pitch needed to seal the reed basket. Jochebed had even included a little canopy for Moses inside the reed basket. She had said to herself, "Perhaps, I will not get to see him under his wedding canopy" (God forbid).

Jochebed has been hiding her son for 3 months from Pharaoh's death decree that every male child at birth MUST be drowned in the Nile. (The same river that Pharaoh wanted to use to drown baby Moses would be the avenue God would use to get him to safety and his next chapter in life.)

Jochebed carefully placed the reed basket that she hand made with painstaking detail in a protected (hidden) area where bushes and reeds grew. She had prayerfully and carefully selected this release site when she made the decision and settled within herself this must be done, and the appointed time had come. She trusted God that this vessel would carry her baby to the other side. She also covered it with much prayer, petition, a heavy heart, faith from every fiber of her being, and tears. She had done everything she possibly could to protect him and make sure he remained alive.[1]

She knew that she HAD to trust God to get her baby to safety without any interference or delays. There was another component involved before her baby could be released in the reed basket that day. Would there be someone there ready and waiting to receive the reed basket upon its arrival that would want to take proper, loving care of him? Miriam (Moses' 6-year old sister) had been instructed by

Jochebed to watch from afar to monitor the safekeeping and certain arrival of the infant Moses in the reed basket.

It was that day, at that appointed time that Pharaoh's daughter, Bithiah, went to bathe at the Nile River edge, as she usually did. Her maidens accompanied her to ensure her safety and privacy. Upon arrival at her favorite bathing spot, Pharaoh's daughter noticed the reed basket floating among the tall river grass nearby. She immediately sent one of her maidens to get the reed basket and bring it to her.

Upon uncovering the reed basket, Pharaoh's daughter discovered infant Moses and he began to cry. Pharaoh's daughter had compassion on him and identified him as one of the Hebrew children. (Paraphrasing Exodus 2:4-10) Little Miriam approached Pharaoh's daughter and inquired, "Shall I go and call to thee a nurse of the Hebrew women, that she may nurse the child for thee?" Pharaoh's daughter said, "Go". At Pharaoh's daughter's instruction, Miriam went and got her Mom to nurse her infant brother Moses. When Jochebed arrived, Pharaoh's daughter instructed her, "Take this child away, and nurse it for me, and I will give thee thy wages". Jochebed took Moses and nursed him.

As infant Moses grew, Jochebed brought him to Pharaoh's daughter and she adopted him as her own son. Pharaoh's daughter named him "Moses". She said she named him Moses because his name meant "I drew him out of the water" ("Drawn Out" or "Set Apart"). Moses was not just "Drawn Out and Set Apart" that day by Pharaoh's daughter out of the Nile to escape Pharaoh's Death Decree, but also to begin the next chapter of his life. Moses was later "Drawn Out and Set Apart" for God's use as an adult to lead the Israelites out of Egypt and through "the Crossover". Moses was also "Drawn Out and Set Apart" for God's use as the "Sent One" after God heard the prayers of the Israelites as they cried out to God during Pharaoh's oppression and injustices while in Egypt.

What is not mentioned in the story when you first read it, is the Unseen Hand that guides and promotes (gently nudges, making certain the precise momentum needed to get the reed basket to its destination is consistently and continuously taking place, making sure that all conditions are met to get infant Moses to his destination at the precise place and time for these events to happen. <u>The Unseen Hand of God</u>.

So goes the journey of life. We are knit in the womb, symbolized by the way Jochebed weaves the reed basket. Carefully and wonderfully made. Then we are launched (born again) to sail and experience the events in between the point of entrance into the world (reed basket being placed in the river) with God's Unseen Hand guiding us and providing momentum and direction as-needed to get us to the other side (to Heaven for those who have asked/received Jesus in their heart to be their Lord and Savior). At Heaven's Gate, God Himself is waiting for us. He looks forward to the day when we meet Him face-to-face to join Him, to take care of us and spend eternity with Him.

Meanwhile, THE CONNECTION, which is Jesus, has paid the price for us to 1) pray to God, 2) walk and talk with God daily as Adam and Eve did before the fall of mankind in the Garden of Eden, and 3) build a one-on-one relationship with God. Without Jesus first having died on the cross and paid the price, we could not do ANY of these things with God, the Creator.

In addition, Jesus is sitting at the right hand of God forever making intercession for us. We are continuously covered with prayer by Jesus and our loved ones (grandparents, moms, dads, pastors, believing spouses, siblings, friends, etc.).

Prayer: Lord Jesus, forgive my sins and come into my heart. Be my Lord and Savior. I renounce Satan and every evil work and wicked way. I give you my life and ask you to guide me into all truths. Holy Spirit I receive you now. Help me to hear God's voice clearly every time He speaks to me in Jesus' name. Amen.

Chapter Two

Moses Had No Clue

Moses had no clue that God had big plans for him to lead the Israelites out of Egypt 80 years later. He had already traveled through one divine "crossover" experience as a three-month-old infant, defying Pharaoh. Now God would use him to not only defy Pharaoh (the most powerful ruler of the world at that time), but to get the Israelites where they needed to be at the exact time they needed to be there to "crossover" the Red Sea on dry land. Both feats of unimaginable, unthinkable odds and miraculous accomplishments. Moses would be one of the few humans to ever speak to God and have a one-on-one relationship with God in the Old Testament. God spoke to others in dreams and visions, but he spoke face-to-face with Moses. Moses was the only one God allowed to see "His back" when He passed by (because of sin, no one could look upon God's face and not die).

It wasn't a coincidence that God used someone who could have died as a three-month-old infant to deliver the Israelites out of the hand of Pharaoh. It wasn't a coincidence that God used someone who had a speech impediment (stammering) to go to speak to Pharaoh and make God's requirement known. It wasn't a coincidence when God caused Moses' staff (walking cane) to turn into a serpent, then turn the serpent back into Moses' staff. Wouldn't you have freaked out if God used you to do those kinds of miracles? I know I would never have been the same!

Moses had no clue that the Israelites would turn on him! He had no clue that it was only a matter of time before the very people God used him to lead in an escape from Pharaoh would blame and accuse him of putting them in danger of being killed! Once the Israelites left Egypt and were cornered by Pharaoh closing in on them, they turned on Moses! It wasn't a coincidence that God used Moses' staff (walking cane) to part the Red Sea. Then God used the same staff to cause the Red Sea to close in on Pharaoh and his army, annihilating (drowning) every one of them with one move. Small is mighty in the Unseen Hand of the Living God! Even when you don't see it, it's working. Even when you don't feel it, it's working. God never stops working. Delivering the oppressed, healing the sick, mending the broken-hearted, working miracles, sparing us from untold danger, destruction, death, wrecks, accidents, illnesses, plagues, and retaliations.

Moses had no clue that God predestined him to have "that kind of relationship with God". That kind of one-on-one relationship with God that would use Moses to work miracles to destroy armies, enemies, plagues, injustices (seen and unseen).

Moses had no clue that God would establish a covenant with him three days after the Red Sea Miracle, when there was no water in Marah.

Exodus 15:26: *IF thou wilt diligently hearken to the voice of the Lord thy God, and wilt do that which is right in His sight, and wilt give ear to His commandments, and keep ALL His statutes, I will put none of these diseases upon thee, which I have brought upon the Egyptians: for I AM the Lord that healeth thee.*

Moses never dreamed God would use him to chisel out (etched in stone) the Ten Commandments on stone tablets while God dictated them to him. God would use Moses to deliver the Ten Commandments to the Israelites and all of creation to live by all the days of their lives. The supreme set of rules to supersede all laws to be passed by rulers, legislation, and world leaders from that moment forward.

Moses had no clue that God would use him to help the Israelite people as a nation (said to have population of 3 million at the time of crossing) to build their relationship with God during a time when no one else would, because they didn't have one-on-one audience with God.

Moses had "that kind of relationship" with God!

Chapter Three

Purpose, Dreams, Potential, Passion

God deposits purpose, dreams, potential and passion into each of us when He knits us in the womb. This should resonate in you to your core, touching and igniting your deepest longings and all of who you are, as well as all of what is in you to be!

It has been said that purpose meets passion later in our lives. The truth is that purpose met passion when God created us and made those deposits in us while knitting us in the womb. He wired and connected purpose to passion (purpose met passion) at that moment. What we experience when we think "passion meets purpose" in life, is our own realization "aha moment" of what God fused together and placed in motion in us before we were born.

Purpose

Once God deposits Purpose into us, He then equips us with everything we need to accomplish our purpose here on earth. Without purpose, life becomes mundane and meaningless. That's why people who either don't know their purpose or forget and get distracted from their purpose get into trouble. They begin to question their reason for living!

> *People who either don't know their purpose or forget and get distracted from their purpose get into trouble. They begin to question their reason for living!*

Our purpose includes spiritual giftings and callings specifically deposited and assigned to us by God. Our purpose includes having a personal relationship with God (walking and talking with Him daily). Our purpose also includes helping others to reach their destinies and get through this life journey. (As we help others, God makes sure our needs get met). Our purpose includes making a positive difference on earth while leaving a legacy for our family, friends, loved ones and all whose lives we touch on the way to Heaven!

God wants me to speak peace to your purpose. God wants each of us to stabilize and do something every day to nurture the seed of our purpose to make sure it grows and becomes stronger, making sure that training and development take place. Every day, we are to be reaching out to others of same craft, skill, industry and/or beliefs. Work was never meant to be your purpose or the meaning for your life. Work is only a result of your life, a piece of the big picture, of what you have done while on earth! Think about it, God speaks to us and deals with the eternal things (things that last forever).

> *Work was never meant to be your purpose or the meaning for your life.*

Now the question is, "Are you going to grow and nurture that seed, or squash it and forget it?" That seed of Purpose needs Dreams, Potential and Passion to endure all the things that pop up during life's journey. It doesn't "just happen".

> **<u>Hosea 4:6:</u>** *My people are destroyed for lack of knowledge. Because you have rejected knowledge, I also will reject you from being priest for Me; Because you have forgotten the law of your God, I also will forget your children.*

We see here that God holds us responsible and accountable to Him not only for our sake, but additionally for our children's sake! That is a major responsibility! He says "Destroy". He didn't say we would have a bad day, bad week or even a bad month. He said destroy! He also lets us know if we lose our vision, we choose destruction!

You may think that because of all you've been through (even the mistakes you have made) that you've missed your purpose or cannot possibly reach your destiny(ies). God is using everything you are going through (and have been through) to 1) shape you into who He (predestined) wants you to be, 2) get you to where you need to go; and 3) prepare/position you to help someone else that is going through the same thing or worse experiences to get through their rough time (test) and reach their destiny(ies).

IT doesn't matter what your last name is, where you were born, how much money you have (or don't have) in your bank account, what you have done or have not done so far in your life. Right where you are, God will use you. If you just yield and allow Him to use you, you will be blessed and protected. While helping someone else, your need gets met. Your situation gets fixed and resolved. Your emotional condition becomes stabilized, you gain emotional strength and are restored (better than before). Your outlook on life is

> *Right where you are, God will use you.*

brightened. You are encouraged. You are reminded that this is a "Small thing for God". God has a purpose and a plan for EVERYTHING you go through in life. He is working it all together for your good AND for the good of those who are (and will be) blessed (helped and encouraged) by you.

Don't have a clue what your purpose is yet? It's never too late! God will cause you to do more in less time (If you Pray and Ask).

<u>Prayer</u>: Holy Spirit reveal to me what is my purpose. Help me to spend the rest of my life walking in that purpose, developing and operating in it, so that I will accomplish everything God put me on this earth to accomplish and touch/affect ALL the lives You put me on this earth to affect and help. Holy Spirit HELP ME to hear clearly from God moment-to-moment, every day of my life, in Jesus' name I pray. Amen.

Dreams

Your dreams are deposited in you by God. Merriam-webster online dictionary defines dreams as: <u>a strongly desired goal or purpose</u>[3]. (I'm not referring to the dreams you receive during your sleep). Dreams, hopes and aspirations are directly connected to your purpose and your potential. Many of the components you have been equipped with in your potential are linked to your dreams. Dreams spark and feed (continuously fueling) your passion. How bad do you want it?

> ***Proverbs 29:28 (KJV):*** *Where there is no vision, the people perish: but he that keepeth the law, happy is he.*

We also know that dreams serve to keep you satisfied, fulfilled, and moving you in the direction of your purpose. Dreams don't just accompany you but see you through to accomplishment and completion of your purpose, your callings, your destiny(ies).

<u>Prayer:</u> I speak to the dreams deposited in me by God when He created me. I speak life to the dry bones. I command the dry bones (unfulfilled dreams) to live again and manifest, accomplishing all that God intended them to be and do when He deposited (placed) them in me in Jesus' name. I command my dreams to exceed what I could dream or imagine, while glorifying God and advancing His kingdom in Jesus' name.

Potential

Our potential is directly and proportionally deposited in us to equip us for everything our purpose will require of us to carry out during this lifetime. God knows exactly everything we need to get the job done for ALL He intends us to do and ALL He intends us to be while here on earth. When God the Father, Jesus the Son, and the Holy Spirit looks at each of us, first they see the blood of Jesus that atoned everything for us and qualifies us to be looked upon and used by the Trinity deity. Then, Father, Son and Holy Spirit see the Potential that God Himself deposited in us to get every aspect of the job done.

As we begin each day, we are to pray that the Holy Spirit will show us (reveal) to us what to do and how to go about it throughout the day and what to pray during that day. Only the Holy Spirit knows what God wants done each day (and what is at the root of every situation and problem) along the way.

Did you know that it grieves God when we do not live our lives to its fullest potential? When we do not live as God intended, His heart is saddened.

Think about it, the Lord's Prayer instructs us to do this, "Give us this day our daily bread". Our daily bread can initially be interpreted as physical food, but spiritual food is included.

In **_Matthew 4:4:_** *But He answered and said, "It is written, 'Man does not live by bread alone, but by EVERY word that proceeds from the mouth of God'."*

Now that's a daily request and a daily need!

Exodus 36:2: *And Moses called Bezaleel and Aholiab and every wise hearted man, in whose heart the Lord had put wisdom, even everyone whose heart stirred him up to come unto the work to do it.*

<u>The potential God placed in us before birth will stir us up to do what He put us on this earth to do.</u>

God wants us to thrive, not just survive. We are to fan the flames of our potential, making sure that every day is better than the previous one. *"Tou Jour Mieu"* as we say in French. This means "every day better" (than the previous one). Not only is potential for our purpose deposited in us when we are knit in the womb, but new creativity is given to us as we spend time with God!

Passion (Determination, Ambition, Zeal)

God deposits, then equips with passion (determination, drive, ambition, zeal) for each step of the process it takes to get the job done. During certain times or phases of the project, we become bombarded by life's cares, distractions or major events. These "life care, distractions, and major events" show up in the form of: birth, a death of a loved one, marriage, divorce, career change, new job, loss of job, accidents, illness, and sometimes trivial events that we allow to interfere with what's really important. When that happens, WE need to pray to the Holy Spirit to fan the flames of that drive, zeal, and ambition with Fresh Fire. Fresh Fire ignites the embers. Fresh Fire sparks Fresh interest. Fresh Fire injects creativity and innovative, witty ideas into our minds-wills-emotions (souls). Fresh Fire energizes every aspect of our being—so we are refreshed, illuminated, propelled and compelled to finish what we started. Fresh Fire energizes and jump-starts us to begin the next phase of our project (or chapter of our life) without hesitation, concern or weariness (like none of what we have been through ever affected our energy, determination, drive or zeal)!

Passion also includes encouraging each other along the way. When? As often as you see someone needing encouragement. We have ALL been in a place where we needed encouragement (a smile, a kind word, reassurance, affirmation, someone to pray with us and for us). All of these are forms of encouragement.

There was a time in my life when I was constantly asking God for reassurance. I asked God if that was "normal". His reply was, "I gave Jesus reassurance when He was being baptized in the Holy Spirit. When He came up out of the water, I said to everyone and to all eternity, "This is My Son, in whom I am well pleased". God continued, "If Jesus needed reassurance, why wouldn't you need it, too?"

We are to move forward with zeal, not trudging along. We are also to encourage one another, knowing that at some point, God will send someone to speak into our lives, see about us, make sure we continue with fresh vision, fresh commitment, and fresh determination to complete the vision (discovery, ideas, angles and approaches, untapped markets, circles of influence) that affect our purpose and potential of what the Holy Spirit is showing us or has shown us. I call it "spark your purpose and potential with passion".

Proverbs 29:28: *Where there is no vision, the people perish: but he that keepeth the law, happy is he.*

Last, but not least, Stay Focused! Don't ever lose sight (vision) of your Purpose, Dreams, Potential and Passion!

Prayer: Holy Spirit, Stir up (spark and ignite) the Purpose, Dreams, Potential and Passion (Determination, Drive, Ambition and Zeal) God placed in me before I was born. Help me to be ALL He intends me to be and do ALL He intends me to do <u>every day</u>. Give me fresh vision and creativity in my purpose, dreams, potential and passion. Help me to <u>always</u> see things the way God sees them. Help me to be a Good Steward of ALL my giftings, callings, my Purpose, my Dreams, my Potential and my Passion (Determination, Drive, Ambition and Zeal) ALL the days of my life, in Jesus' name. I ask you to <u>remove all limitations</u> that have been placed on me and my children (family), our purpose, dreams, potential and passion (determination, drive, ambition and zeal) knowingly or unknowingly by me or others through negative talk or actions toward my family in Jesus' name. Thank you for making a way for me and my family to thrive (not just survive) <u>daily</u> in our purpose, dreams, potential, determination, ambition, and zeal in Jesus' name.

Chapter Four

We Need To Log In!

Written in the paradigm of daily computer function, this chapter illuminates how each day we need to log in to God's Presence as directed (not suggested) in Psalms 91:3, 9-12.

__Psalms 91: 3, 9-12:__ [3] Surely he shall deliver thee from the snare of the fowler, and from the noisome pestilence. [9] Because thou hast made the Lord, which is my refuge, even the most High, thy habitation; [10] There shall no evil befall thee, neither shall any plague come nigh thy dwelling. [11] For he shall give his angels charge over thee, to keep thee in all thy ways. [12] They shall bear thee up in their hands, lest thou dash thy foot against a stone.

Turn the page to experience this glorious, enlightening process and transformation!

When We Log In,
God Spares Us from Consequences

Most of us, at some point during our day, log into our computers, our phones, the programs and services that we need to function and move forward. We log in with passwords, pass codes, and fingerprint verification. We log in to get our work done, get our bills paid, get services turned on or cancelled, to move forward with our day (and with our lives). We log in to get our groceries, receive resources, get instructions, communicate with important clients, make appointments and meet our deadlines. During pandemic shutdowns, school and college coursework is being required to continue online. You HAVE TO log into the websites as instructed to complete your daily school lessons and requirements to pass each class. Logging in

> *Logging in produces life changing results.*

produces life changing results. We go through the motions, completing required classwork, homework, and remote work from our jobs with the priority and determination that we MUST get this done today, or there will be consequences.

Guess what? <u>When we don't log into the presence of God, there will be consequences</u>. Daily mounting pressure and tension, unbearable news, misunderstandings, delays, malfunctions, wrong turns, wrong information, overpaying for services, having tests run, or services performed we really don't need!!!

Recently, my hot water heater went out. I was told I would have to purchase a new one. Last time I purchased a water heater it was $150. Now water heaters cost $1500! I didn't have it. The earliest install on a new one was in 3 weeks (delays). Three weeks with cold showers (it was wintertime)—unacceptable! Tension was attempting to mount quickly. I called my HVAC resource. He said the water heater I own has a lifetime warranty on the lining, so all I needed was to replace the elements. He contacted a plumber he works closely with to replace the elements for me. Same day service. The price I paid was 1/10th of what I had been told earlier (wrong information). I avoided overpaying AND avoided installing costly products and services I didn't need. This is just a minor example of the situations and decisions we face daily. God navigates us through and spares us from them. Situations He never intended us to go through.

> *I avoided overpaying AND avoided installing costly products and services I didn't need. CONSEQUENCES*

Serious, life-threatening situations loom around us every day. We have no idea! As long as we are logged into the presence of God daily, He protects us.

Once you have received Jesus as your Lord and Savior (salvation), you NEED to daily log into the presence of God! This connection is your lifeline, protection, security, God's navigation system, forward movement, and stability.

God breathed life into you. The Unseen Hand of God is daily nudging you, guiding you, moving you forward to make sure you get where you need to go every day. God is keeping you out of Unseen dangers, pitfalls, and situations that He never intended you to go through.

<u>Daily login is NECESSARY</u>. How can we expect to move forward at all, or keep the pace and momentum we need to in order to get where WE need to be at the exact moment we need to be there, UNLESS we stay logged into the presence of God?

When we log into the presence of the Master Builder of the universe, He gives us EVERYTHING we need to accomplish what He put us on earth to do (it is released). In His presence, we gain and renew balance and peace in our lives, situations, relationships, and jobs. We need balance and peace in our lives daily/ continuously. Each time you Log In to God's presence, you are transformed! You cannot spend time in God's Presence and not be transformed. The human body cannot help but respond to God's Presence. (Some of us get tingly, some cry, some laugh, some go limp.) As you Log In to God's presence, God will launch you into new things He has for you. This launching, and these new things are only available to those who Log In consistently and spend time in His presence. Since the beginning of time, God has been waiting on each of us to Log In and spend Quality Time (QT) in His Presence. Each of us have been created (born) for companionship (relationship) with God.

> *You NEED to daily log into the presence of God!*

If you wonder how important this is? Well, Jesus died for that! Yeah, you might say, "I thought Jesus died for the forgiveness of our sins". He did. Without the shed blood of Jesus Christ (His death and resurrection), our sins would not have been forgiven, AND, we COULD NOT EVER have a relationship with God! Because where sin is, God's Presence cannot be in the same place. He is Holy. Those who Log In and spend time in God's Presence must be born again (salvation), and praising God to go there. Salvation is believing in God the Father, Jesus the Son, and the Holy Spirit, Three-in-One.

> *Each time you Log In to God's presence, you are transformed!*

When We Log In, God Uses This Time to Repair the Broken Places & Engages You to Let Go of the Past

Sooooo important! It is once we Log In to the Presence of God, God uses this time to repair the broken places. <u>What does a broken place look like</u>? (Mending emotional scars, broken promises, broken hearts, broken minds, broken marriages, broken families, forgive and restore shattered trust, soothe disappointments, erase angry, hurtful words, betrayal from a family member or friend, sabotage, being wronged or taken advantage of by others, neglect, abuse, abandonment, rejection, grief from loss, death, divorce, job; and resentment is dissolved). <u>Without this repair, we limp along</u> different paths of our journey in a fragmented manner with deep past hurts and crippling fear. Past hurts cause us to not reach forward (resentment). Crippling Fear causes us to not move past our past, minimizing our effectiveness. Crippling Fear paralyzes us from moving forward, keeps reminding us of bad experiences, being wronged and failed attempts—holding us back from operating in the higher places and accomplishments/destiny(ies) God has planned for us

(overcoming our challenges). There is no failure in God. That's why He is constantly and continuously turning everything in our lives around for our good!

It is once we Log In to the Presence of God, God engages us in releasing and letting go of the past. Something we MUST do BEFORE we can be launched into the New things, he has for each of us. Moving forward is imperative during each stage of our journey. Getting stuck in the Past is a severe handicap that disables more people than we know, and more than we could dream or imagine. It is as disabling as depression. Even unresolved past issues (regrets) can stop us from moving forward and being launched into the New Things God has for us.

> *Once we Log In to the Presence of God, God engages us in releasing and letting go of the Past*

Logging In to the Presence of God restores wholeness (also included in the balance and peace we need along our journey). Wholeness is necessary in us, so we can be used by God to assist the people He sends across our path, helping them overcome their challenges and reach their destiny along the way.

When We Log In, God Uses This Time to Bring Clarity, Enlightenment, and Positions Us to Steer Clear of Deceptions

When we Log In to presence of God, He releases enlightenment and clarity into our mind, will, and emotions (soul). This includes insight, explanation, direction, and instructions on what to do and how to go about problems, planned or unplanned situations, decision-making, deadlines, assignments, projects, opportunities, and circumstances. This enlightenment and clarity can be for our individual needs or the needs of family, friends, co-workers, and employers.

<u>Logging in to God's presence gives us light even in the middle of ANY darkness.</u>

<u>Psalms 18:28</u> ***For You will light my lamp; The Lord my God will enlighten my darkness.***

When you find yourself in ANY dark place at ANY time—whether it is sudden or temporary confusion, chaos, turmoil, misunderstanding, or life-threatening situation, you need to Log in to the Presence of God through prayer and praise. God's light will immediately give you light and clarity into the situation and show you how to escape the dark place, so it does not escalate or overtake you. Darkness can come in the form of deception (wrong teaching, fake news, distractions-deceptions-ensnared (trapped, caught, entangled)—things that are totally opposite of what we know to be true, good and right.

> *<u>**2 Timothy 3:1-9:**</u> But know this, that in the last days perilous times will come: ² For men will be lovers of themselves, lovers of money, boasters, proud, blasphemers, disobedient to parents, unthankful, unholy, ³ unloving, unforgiving, slanderers, without self-control, brutal, despisers of good, ⁴ traitors, headstrong, haughty, lovers of pleasure rather than lovers of God, ⁵ having a form of godliness but denying its power. And from such people turn away! ⁶ For of this sort are those who creep into households and make captives of gullible women loaded down with sins, led away by various lusts, ⁷ always learning and never able to come to the knowledge of the truth. ⁸ Now as Jannes and Jambres resisted Moses, so do these also resist the truth: men of corrupt minds, disapproved concerning the faith; ⁹ but they will progress no further, for their folly will be manifest to all, as theirs also was.*

I have to go one step further and remind you that deception is also thinking that you can make it in this world without the Way Maker. He is not only the ONE that makes a way where there seems to be no way. He IS THE WAY, the truth, the light, and the life. If we ever get to the point where we think we can get there (anywhere) on our own (without God), we have deceived ourselves! ***<u>John 14:6</u> Jesus said to him, "I am the way, the truth, and the life. No one comes to the Father except through Me.*** The

> *If we ever get to the point where we think we can get there on our own (without God), we have deceived ourselves!*

world system would love to have you think you can make it on your own. Because we are His children, we MUST Log in to make it through the storms, overcome the challenges, through the rough/tough times, through the pandemic times, through isolation and trying times, through good times, even through celebrations. He is right there with us through it ALL. We need to Log In to make sure we don't miss His Way.

Acts 17:28: *"For in Him, we live and move and have our being."*

Matthew 24:24: *For false christs and false prophets will rise and show great signs and wonders to deceive, if possible, even the elect.*

(Even all of us who should know better!) Deceptions will be around us in greater volume than ever before. Deceptions will present themselves in various kinds, shapes, forms, and manners. We will be stunned and astounded at what measures the world system will go to in an attempt to get us "on their side". The communication of those who are deceived is filled with confusion. Scams, fraud, theories, half-truths, bait-and-switch deals, negativity, sensationalism of crises and bad news, projections that play on people's sympathies and fears. Deceptions are always competing for our attention, our support, our time, our energy, our money, our belief and agreement.

> *It is imperative that you KNOW that only God's light can get you through deception and darkness.*

God's word and God's light (received when we Log In to His presence) make it not only do-able (possible), but eases our way (removes the struggle) to get us through whatever darkness we must go through or deception that presents itself.

1 John 1:5: *This is the message which we have heard from*

Him and declare to you, that God is light and in Him is no darkness at all.

It is imperative that you KNOW that only God's light can get you through deception and darkness.

John 8:12: *Then Jesus spoke to them again, saying, "I am the light of the world. He who follows Me shall not walk in darkness but have the light of life."*

Ever been in a place where people believed a lie as though it were the truth? Scary thought, but we are seeing it around us even now! It's called deception (propaganda, fake news, planned shortages, misinformation, blame-game, calling attention to something or someone else to get the attention-focus off the real root of the situation or problem).

Chapter Five

Holy Spirit is the Firewall!

The Holy Spirit is the Firewall that guards the entrance (access) to God's Presence. The Holy Spirit requires honesty and transparency (no pretense or deception, contaminants or pollution allowed) in the hearts of any who attempt to Log In to the presence of God.

Hebrews 10:19-22: *Therefore, brethren, having boldness to enter the Holiest by the blood of Jesus, [20] by a new and living way which He consecrated for us, through the veil, that is, His flesh, [21] and having a High Priest over the house of God, [22] let us draw near with a true heart in full assurance of faith, having our hearts sprinkled from an evil conscience and our bodies washed with pure water.*

When we Log In to God's presence, we MUST seek His face and Quality Time with Him, not so that we can bring Him our To-Do prayer list. We worship Him, listen for what He is telling us, and pray according to what the Holy Spirit tells us. During this Log In time we discover and learn God's priorities, not ours. It is during this Log In time, God shows us the difference between God's Truth and man's philosophies in whatever situation, storm, decision, deception we are facing and dealing with.

The Holy Spirit draws you into God's Presence. The Holy Spirit draws you through prayer (talking to God), praise and worship (thanking God, singing to God, or dancing with tambourines), desperation for a need or situation in your life or the life of a loved one.

When we are Logged In to the Presence of God, the Holy Spirit MOVES US.

> ***Ezekiel 1:20:*** *Wherever the spirit wanted to go, they went, because there the spirit went; and the wheels were lifted together with them, <u>for the spirit of the living creatures was in the wheels.</u>*

Chapter Six

God Miraculously Turned the Storm!

When I was growing up in Louisiana, severe hurricanes would come through our region often during hurricane season. Almost every time, we would have cousins that would come to our house to stay until the hurricane passed. They lived in Franklin, Louisiana in homes located in lower lying flood zones.

During the fiercest parts of the hurricane we would all assemble in the dining room), get on our knees and pray. Because we were Catholics, we would pray the rosary. Mom and Dad would add their own special prayers as God lead them to pray for special needs, such as protection, peace, sparing any damage to our home, our crops, the homes of all assembled and their extended families.

Later in life, we were preparing for a hurricane forecasted to hit our community. I mentioned to my Dad that I had prayed that God would spare us from any damage of the storm as it was projected to hit our location. My Dad asked me if I had ever thought about praying that God would cause the storm to turn its path and not come where we were. I prayed the prayer Dad suggested. God honored/answered the prayer and the hurricane turned its path!

In October, 2002, Category 4 Hurricane Lili was projected to hit Lafayette, Louisiana and destroy all in its path. I was living in Georgia at that time. My sister called me with great anxiety. Her voice shook as she explained to me this major Hurricane was headed straight toward where they lived. She pleaded with me to pray that God would cause the storm to turn away from Lafayette and Acadia parishes. We stood in agreement in prayer on the phone, then I continued to pray through to the breakthrough.

I remember her describing the events during our next visit, saying, "It came up the Vermilion river toward us. No hurricane has ever left the Gulf Coast, then travelled up an inland waterway in this part of Louisiana. Then…it weakened and turned. That was a miracle!" My God comes through even in the midst of the fiercest of storms. My nephew remembers they had to purchase a generator to have electricity. Due to the major storm damage and power outages throughout the area, the electrical utility company did not restore electricity to their home for 6 weeks. Imagine being without full electrical power for 6 weeks! However, we were all thankful everyone at their house survived the hurricane.

[2] The paragraph below and the chart on the following page are excerpts from the National Weather Service Report of Hurricane Lili dated October 2, 2002, showing the projected path of the storm (and exactly where it turned). The report also states that the storm

unexpectedly weakened, then turned right before it reached the location in the corner of Lafayette and Acadia parishes where my sister lived.

"Lili countered preparedness moves with an unexpected and threatening intensification to winds of 145 mph, making it a Category IV hurricane. With Lili located only 200 miles south of Intracoastal City, Louisiana, officials had to act fast and brace for the worst. By the early evening hours on the 2nd (October, 2002), the National Hurricane Center adjusted the track of the storm with landfall 50 miles east of the previous forecast track. This put Lili on a direct course into Vermilion Parish, potentially ushering in a deadly storm surge of 18 to 20 feet across Vermilion Bay.

During the pre-dawn hours of the 3rd (October, 2002), tensions ran high as Lili moved northwest as forecast. However, an unexpected twist made all the difference between life and death as Lili began to weaken. Satellite imagery began to reveal that the eyewall was filling. At daybreak on the 3rd (October, 2002), Lili was downgraded to a Category II storm with winds of only 100 mph."

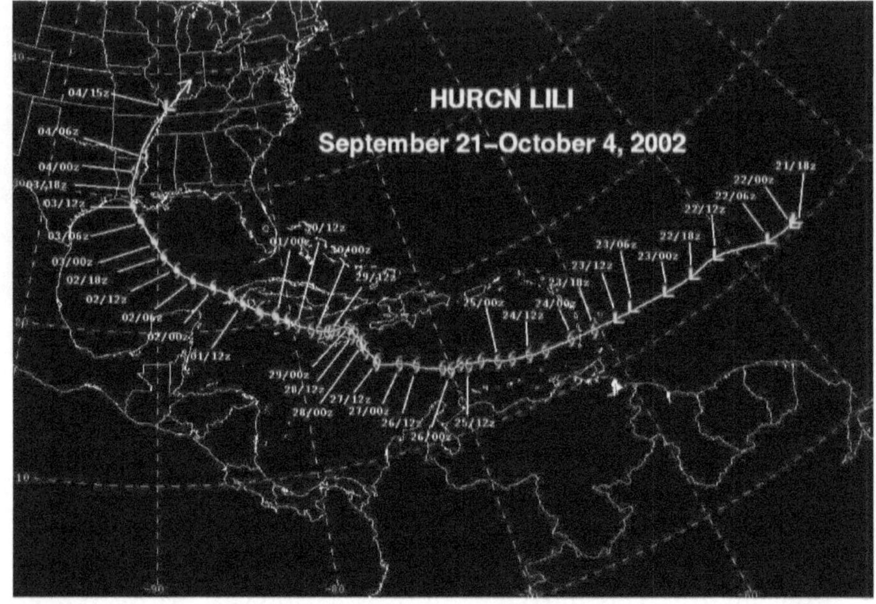
HURCN LILI
September 21–October 4, 2002

Chapter Seven

Journey to Heaven

The <u>Unseen Hand of God</u> is constantly and consistently beckoning us, navigating (guiding) us, gently propelling us in His perfect timing to do and accomplish what we must do in order to reach the "Other Side". Just like God did with Moses when he was in the reed basket. <u>Nothing that takes place during our lifetime is coincidence.</u> God knows it all before we are born. God loves us so much that He even turns our mistakes and failures into blessings. He turns everything along the way (during life's journey) around for our good, in spite of us or others who try to knowingly or unknowingly delay and/or derail us from accomplishing what God put us on earth to accomplish before we get to be with Him for eternity. And NOTHING can separate us from the love of God EVER.

<u>Romans 8:38:</u> *For I am persuaded that neither death nor life, nor angels nor principalities nor powers, nor things present nor* *things to come, [39] nor height nor depth, nor any other created thing, shall be able to separate us from the love of God which is in Christ Jesus our Lord.*

Then, when it's God's time for us to go home to meet Him, He prepares and strengthens us for "the crossover" and stands on the "other side", waiting to receive us there. Just like the nursemaid was waiting on the "other side" for Moses' arrival that eventful day.

Joshua 3:7: *And the Lord said to Joshua, "This day I will begin to exalt you in the sight of all Israel, that they may know that, <u>as I was with Moses, so I will be with you</u>."*

It was all according to God's plans and purposes being accomplished on this earth with the Unseen Hand of God gently guiding Moses (and us) along until we meet Him in Heaven. You know the scripture. He has prepared a place for us. A mansion with many rooms, where the streets are made of gold. A place where there is no sorrow, no crying, no pain, no sickness, no struggling or hardships, no pandemics, no suffering, no loneliness.

> *And NOTHING can separate us from the love of God EVER.*

More Information

<u>Visit My website</u>

For more information concerning Motivational Seminars, Speaking Engagements, and Book Signing Events for your business, church, youth or civic group, please visit my website at www.highersuccesstoday.com

Available on the website: Book Purchasing Options, Weekly Blog, and Event Schedules (In-Person or Virtual).

<u>Contact</u>

Email: Lrichard@highersuccesstoday.com

<u>Published Works by Lona Richard</u>

Higher Levels of Success

Unseen Hand of God

Endnotes

[1] Kadari, Tamar. "Jochebed: Midrash and Aggadah." Jewish Women's Archive. https://jwa.org/encyclopedia/article/jochebed-midrash-and-aggadah (accessed March 2, 2020).

[2] "Dream." Merriam-Webster Online Dictionary. https://www.merriam-webster.com/dictionary/dream (accessed May 5, 2020).

[3] Kuyper, Kent, Marty Mayeaux, Donovan Landreneau, and Joe Rua. n.d. "HURRICANE LILI." https://www.weather.gov/media/lch/events/lili.pdf. (accessed July 10, 2020).

www.ingramcontent.com/pod-product-compliance
Lightning Source LLC
Chambersburg PA
CBHW022043050726
47591CB00003B/923